THE RESCUED YEAR

Books by William Stafford

The Rescued Year

Traveling through the Dark

West of Your City

THE RESCUED YEAR

by William Stafford

1817

HARPER & ROW, PUBLISHERS

NEW YORK, EVANSTON, AND LONDON

STANDARD BOOK NUMBER: 06-013963-3

LIBRARY OF CONGRESS CATALOG CARD NUMBER: *66-20746*

76 77 78 79 10 9 8 7 6 5 4 3

ACKNOWLEDGMENTS

Acknowledgment is made to the following magazines, in which some of these poems have previously appeared:

The Atlantic Monthly for "Fifteen" and "The Animal That Drank Up Sound"
Botteghe Oscure for "For the Grave of Daniel Boone"
The Carleton Miscellany for "Once Men Were Created"
Colorado Quarterly for "Doubt on the Great Divide"
Compass Review for "Some Shadows"
The Critical Quarterly for "A Documentary from America" and "Near Edinburgh Castle"
FOCUS/Midwest for "My Father: October 1942" and "Right Now"
The Goodly Co for "The Epitaph Ending in And"
Granta for "Aunt Mabel"
Harper's Magazine for "Judgments" and "Keepsakes"
MSS for "Passing Remark" and "At the Klamath Berry Festival"
The New York Times for "The Tulip Tree" and "Hunting"
Nimrod for "Winterward"
The Northwest Review for "Back Home" and "Believer"
The Paris Review for "Recoil"
The Pioneer Log for "Sophocles Says"
Poetry for "Across Kansas," "The Rescued Year," "Our City Is Guarded by Automatic Rockets," "Following the *Markings* of Dag Hammarskjöld," "A Human Condition" and "Near"
Poetry Northwest for "Homecoming," "At the Fair," "Across the Lake's Eye" and "Read to the Last Line"
Saturday Review for "Uncle George," "Strokes," "When I Was Young" and "Out West"
The Southern Review for "A Farewell in Tumbleweed Time"
The Virginia Quarterly Review for "From Eastern Oregon"
Western Review for "At the Chairman's Housewarming"
The Western Humanities Review for "Letter from Oregon"

The following poems appeared in *West of Your City* (The Talisman Press, 1960): "One Home," "Vacation," "The Farm on the Great Plains," "Listening," "The Well Rising," "At the Bomb Testing Site," "In the Deep Channel," "Connections," "The Fish Counter at Bonneville," "Walking West," "Our People," "Bi-focal," "Ice Fishing" and "The Move to California."

CONTENTS

III

IV

I

The Tulip Tree

Many a winter night
the green of the tulip tree
lives again among other trees,
returns through miles of rain
to that level of color
all day pattered, wind-wearied,
calmly asserted in our yard.

Only pale by the evergreen,
hardly distinguished by leaf or color,
it used to slide a little pale from other trees,
and—no great effect at our house—
it sustained what really belonged
but would, if severely doubted,
disappear.

Many a winter night
it arrives and says for a moment:
"I am still here."

Some Shadows

You would not want too reserved a speaker—
that is a cold way to live.
But where I come from withdrawal
is easy to forgive.

When Mother was a girl Indians
shadowed that country, the barren lands.
Mother ran to school winter mornings
with hot potatoes in her hands.

She was like this—foreign, a stranger.
She could not hear very well;
the world was all far. (Were the others laughing?
She never could tell.)

Later, though she was frightened,
she loved, like everyone.
A lean man, a cruel, took her.
I am his son.

He was called Hawk by the town people,
but was an ordinary man.
He lived by trapping and hunting
wherever the old slough ran.

Our house was always quiet.
Summers the windmill creaked, or a board.
I carried wood, never touching anyone.
Winters the black stove roared.

Forgive me these shadows I cling to, good people,
trying to hold quiet in my prologue.
Hawks cling the barrens wherever I live.
The world says, "Dog eat dog."

Across Kansas

My family slept those level miles
but like a bell rung deep till dawn
I drove down an aisle of sound,
nothing real but in the bell,
past the town where I was born.

Once you cross a land like that
you own your face more: what the light
struck told a self; every rock
denied all the rest of the world.
We stopped at Sharon Springs and ate—

My state still dark, my dream too long to tell.

My Father: October 1942

He picks up what he thinks is
a road map, and it is
his death: he holds it easily, and
nothing can take it from his firm hand.
The pulse in his thumb on the map
says, "1:19 P.M. next Tuesday, at
this intersection." And an ambulance
begins to throb while his face looks tired.

Any time anyone may pick up something
so right that he can't put it down:
that is the problem for all who travel—they
fatally own whatever is really theirs,
and that is the inner thread, the lock,
what can hold. If it is to be, nothing breaks
it. Millions of observers guess all the
time, but each person, once, can say, "Sure."

Then he's no longer an observer. He isn't right,
or wrong. He just wins or loses.

Back Home

The girl who used to sing in the choir
would have a slow shadow on dependable walls,
I saw. We walked summer nights.
Persons came near in those days,
both afraid but not able to know
anything but a kind of Now.

In the maples an insect sang
insane for hours about how deep the dark was.
Over the river, past the light on the bridge,
and then where the light quelled at limits
in the park, we left the town,
the church lagging pretty far behind.

When I went back I saw many sharp things:
the wild hills coming to drink at the river,
the church pondering its old meanings.
I believe the hills won; I am afraid
the girl who used to sing in the choir
broke into jagged purple glass.

A Family Turn

All her Kamikaze friends admired my aunt,
their leader, charmed in vinegar,
a woman who could blaze with such white blasts
as Lawrence's that lit Arabia.
Her mean opinions bent her hatpins.

We'd take a ride in her old car
that ripped like Sherman through society:
Main Street's oases sheltered no one
when she pulled up at Thirty-first
and whirled that Ford for another charge.

We swept headlines from under rugs, names
all over town, which I learned her way, by heart,
and blazed with love that burns because it's real.
With a turn that's our family's own,
she'd say, "Our town is not the same"—

Pause—"And it's never been."

Fifteen

South of the bridge on Seventeenth
I found back of the willows one summer
day a motorcycle with engine running
as it lay on its side, ticking over
slowly in the high grass. I was fifteen.

I admired all that pulsing gleam, the
shiny flanks, the demure headlights
fringed where it lay; I led it gently
to the road and stood with that
companion, ready and friendly. I was fifteen.

We could find the end of a road, meet
the sky on out Seventeenth. I thought about
hills, and patting the handle got back a
confident opinion. On the bridge we indulged
a forward feeling, a tremble. I was fifteen.

Thinking, back farther in the grass I found
the owner, just coming to, where he had flipped
over the rail. He had blood on his hand, was pale—
I helped him walk to his machine. He ran his hand
over it, called me good man, roared away.

I stood there, fifteen.

The Rescued Year

Take a model of the world so big
it is the world again, pass your hand,
press back that area in the west where no one lived,
the place only your mind explores. On your thumb
that smudge becomes my ignorance, a badge
the size of Colorado: toward that state by train
we crossed our state like birds and lodged—
the year my sister gracefully
grew up—against the western boundary
where my father had a job.

Time should go the way it went
that year: we weren't at war; we had
each day a treasured unimportance;
the sky existed, so did our town;
the library had books we hadn't read;
every day at school we learned and sang,
or at least hummed and walked in the hall.

In church I heard the preacher; he said
"Honor!" with a sound like empty silos
repeating the lesson. For a minute I held
Kansas Christian all along the Santa Fe.
My father's mean attention, though, was busy—this
I knew—and going home his wonderfully level gaze
would hold the state I liked, where little happened
and much was understood. I watched my father's finger
mark off huge eye-scans of what happened in the creed.

Like him, I tried. I still try,
send my sight like a million pickpockets
up rich people's drives: it is time

when I pass for every place I go to be alive.
Around any corner my sight is a river,
and I let it arrive: rich by those brooks
his thought poured for hours
into my hand. His creed: the greatest ownership
of all is to glance around and understand.

That Christmas Mother made paper
presents; we colored them with crayons
and hung up a tumbleweed for a tree.
A man from Hugoton brought my sister
a present (his farm was tilted near oil
wells; his car ignored the little
bumps along our drive: nothing
came of all this—it was just part of the year).

I walked out where a girl I knew would be;
we crossed the plank over the ditch
to her house. There was popcorn on the stove,
and her mother recalled the old days, inviting me back.
When I walked home in the cold evening,
snow that blessed the wheat had roved
along the highway seeking furrows,
and all the houses had their lights—
oh, that year did not escape me: I rubbed
the wonderful old lamp of our dull town.

That spring we crossed the state again,
my father soothing us with stories:
the river lost in Utah, underground—
"They've explored only the ones they've found!"—
and that old man who spent his life knowing,
unable to tell how he knew—
"I've been sure by smoke, persuaded
by mist, or a cloud, or a name:

once the truth was ready"—my father smiled
at this—"it didn't care how it came."

In all his ways I hold that rescued year—
comes that smoke like love into the broken
coal, that forms to chunks again and lies
in the earth again in its dim folds, and comes a sound,
then shapes to make a whistle fade,
and in the quiet I hold no need, no hurry:
any day the dust will move, maybe settle;
the train that left will roll back into our station,
the name carved on the platform unfill with rain,
and the sound that followed the couplings back
will ripple forward and hold the train.

Homecoming

Under my hat I custom you intricate, Ella;
at homecoming I glance and remember your street.
"What happened to Ella?" they ask, asking too fast;
so I fold them off, thousands of answers deep.

"Nobody saw her after the war." We are driving;
in front of the Union Building we stop and get out.
You balanced one night on that step, then leaned.
"There's Potter's Lake." And there goes our path down straight.

"Hello, Paul." "Howdy, Tom." "Glad to see you again."
They shake. "It's been a long time," they bellow, "by God!"
I shake. They sing an old song. I hunt a face.
Every voice yells in my ear, "She's married or dead."

Oh all you revelers, back of the songs you're singing
they have torn down Ella's house—you've forgotten it;
and Ella is lost, who brightened all our class,
and I stand here, home-come, to celebrate.

Under my hat I custom you intricate, Ella,
passing the places, betraying them all with a wave,
adding past dates and jobs that led us apart
flickering into revolving doors, till I've

Lost you. What happened to Ella? Where does she live?
Remember, Tom? She's that girl we once spoke of.

Judgments

I accuse—
    Ellen: you have become forty years old,
    and successful, tall, well-groomed,
    gracious, thoughtful, a secretary.
    Ellen, I accuse.

George—
    You know how to help others;
    you manage a school. You never
    let fear or pride or faltering plans
    break your control.
    George, I accuse.

I accuse—
    Tom: you have found a role;
    now you meet all kinds of people
    and let them find the truth of your
    eminence; you need not push.
    Oh, Tom, I do accuse.

Remember—
    The gawky, hardly to survive students
    we were: not one of us going to succeed,
    all of us abjectly aware of how cold,
    unmanageable the real world was?
    I remember. And that fear was true.
    And is true.

Last I accuse—
    Myself: my terrible poise, knowing
    even this, knowing that then we
    sprawled in the world

and were ourselves part of it; now
we hold it firmly away with gracious
gestures (like this of mine!) we've achieved.

I see it all too well—
    And I am accused, and I accuse.

Uncle George

Some catastrophes are better than others.
Wheat under the snow lived by blizzards
that massacred stock on Uncle George's farm.
Only telephone poles remember the place, and the wire
thrills a mile at a time into that intent blast
where the wind going by fascinated whole
millions of flakes and thousands of acres of tumbleweeds.

There in the spring birds will come measuring along
their nesting stream where I like to go hunt through the snow
for furred things that wait and survive. Trapper
of warm sight, I plow and belong, send breath
to be part of the day, and where it arrives
I spend on and on, fainter and fainter
toward ultimate identification, joining the air
a few breaths at a time. I test a bough
that held, last year, but this year may come down.

The cold of Uncle George's farm I carry home in my
overcoat, where I live reluctantly one life at a time;
like one driven on, I flutter, measure my stream
by many little calls: "Oh, Uncle George—where you
poured the chicken feed!—where you broke open
the window screen for the nesting swallow!—where the barn
held summer and winter against that slow blizzard, the sky!"

Aunt Mabel

This town is haunted by some good deed
that reappears like a country cousin, or truth
when language falters these days trying to lie,
because Aunt Mabel, an old lady gone now, would
accost even strangers to give bright flowers
away, quick as a striking snake. It's deeds like this
have weakened me, shaken by intermittent trust,
stricken with friendliness.

Our Senator talked like war, and Aunt Mabel
said, "He's a brilliant man,
but we didn't elect him that much."

Everyone's resolve weakens toward evening
or in a flash when a face melds—a stranger's, even—
reminded for an instant between menace and fear:
There are Aunt Mabels all over the world,
      or their graves in the rain.

One Home

Mine was a Midwest home—you can keep your world.
Plain black hats rode the thoughts that made our code.
We sang hymns in the house; the roof was near God.

The light bulb that hung in the pantry made a wan light,
but we could read by it the names of preserves—
outside, the buffalo grass, and the wind in the night.

A wildcat sprang at Grandpa on the Fourth of July
when he was cutting plum bushes for fuel,
before Indians pulled the West over the edge of the sky.

To anyone who looked at us we said, "My friend";
liking the cut of a thought, we could say, "Hello."
(But plain black hats rode the thoughts that made our code.)

The sun was over our town; it was like a blade.
Kicking cottonwood leaves we ran toward storms.
Wherever we looked the land would hold us up.

Strokes

The left side of her world is gone—
the rest sustained by memory
and a realization: There are still the children.

Going down our porch steps her pastor
calls back: "We are proud of her recovery,
and there is a chiropractor up in Galesburg. . . ."

The birthdays of the old require such candles.

Our City Is Guarded by Automatic Rockets

1.
Breaking every law except the one
for Go, rolling its porpoise way, the rocket
staggers on its course; its feelers lock
a stranglehold ahead; and—rocking—finders
whispering "Target, Target," back and forth,
relocating all its meaning in the dark,
it freezes on the final stage. I know
that lift and pour, the flick out of the sky
and then the power. Power is not enough.

2.
Bough touching bough, touching . . . till the shore,
a lake, an undecided river, and a lake again
saddling the divide: a world that won't be wise
and let alone, but instead is found outside
by little channels, linked by chance, not stern;
and then when once we're sure we hear a guide
it fades away toward the opposite end of the road
from home—the world goes wrong in order to have revenge.
Our lives are an amnesty given us.

3.
There is a place behind our hill so real
it makes me turn my head, no matter. There
in the last thicket lies the cornered cat
saved by its claws, now ready to spend
all there is left of the wilderness, embracing
its blood. And that is the way that I will spit
life, at the end of any trail where I smell any hunter,
because I think our story should not end—
or go on in the dark with nobody listening.

Believer

A horse could gallop over our bridge that minnows
used for shade, but our dog trotting would splinter
that bridge—"Look down," my father said, and there
went Buster to break that bridge, but I called him back
that day:—whatever they ask me to believe, "And
    furthermore," I say.

At Niagara one night in a motel I woke, and this is what I saw—
on their little pallets all our kids lay scattered over
the floor, their dreams overcome by the story we live,
and I awake in that spell. Since then, every night
I leap through doubt, eager to find
    many more truths to tell.

And scared as I am with my blood full of sharks, I lie
in the dark and believe that whistle our dog's ears could hear
but no one else heard—it skewers my dream; and in crystals
finer than frost I trace and accept all of the ways
to know:—they tell me a lie; I don't say "But"—
    there are ways for a lie to be so.

You don't hear me yell to test the quiet or try to shake
the wall, for I understand that the wrong sound weakens
what no sound could ever save, and I am the one
to live by the hum that shivers till the world can sing:—
May my voice hover and wait for fate,
    when the right note shakes everything.

Letter from Oregon

Mother, here there are shadowy salmon;
ever their sides argue up the falls.
Watching them plunge with fluttering gills,
I thought back through Wyoming where I came from.

The gleaming sides of my train glimmered
up over passes and arrowed through shoals
of aspen fluttering in a wind of yellow.
Only the sky stayed true; I turned,

Justifying space through those miles of Wyoming
till the wave of the land was quelled by the stars;
then tunnels of shadow led me far
through doubt, and I was home.

Mother, even home was doubtful;
many slip into the sea and are gone for years,
just as I boarded the six-fifteen there.
Over the bar I have leaped outward.

Somewhere in the ocean beyond Laramie
when that grass folded low in the dark
a lost fin waved, and I felt the beat
of the old neighborhood stop, on our street.

Vacation

One scene as I bow to pour her coffee: —

> Three Indians in the scouring drouth
> huddle at a grave scooped in the gravel,
> lean to the wind as our train goes by.
> Someone is gone.
> There is dust on everything in Nevada.

I pour the cream.

A Farewell in Tumbleweed Time

One after another, fish fast over the fence
and quick roll to rebound, lost summer
marshaled her ragged bushy-haired children;
and pell-mell for winter, into our starved light
the west blizzard harried bigger Attila tumbleweeds
driven down what became a canyon
wherever you looked and what stood silvery
gray leaning upward—the part of the storm
you could see, your movable cell, a wild prison.

Our house then, disguised to be any house, outwaited
the storm; our mailbox in sunlight held
level; our gate steadied by shadow performed
a scenario. But into it years came, and then all that
bravery everyone praised good people for
was the wrong thing: nothing changed fast, but moss
muted every brick with its message, while
vines tried to find our grandparents' weaknesses
all up the tall chimney.

I was going to come back some day
after the fragments and I found a new home
and offer to the indifferent air a secret
no one there could use at the time:
about four some winter's day, somewhere
roads don't go, where hills come down,
I'd hold out the unfinished years of our life
and call for the steadfast rewards we were promised.
I'd speak for all the converging days of our town.

Then it would be like the flood of Christmas that
preserved every stone and set all the stars on the hill

where the farm leaned when we came out Main Street
with so much richness we couldn't ever give it away.
But all the rest of this time, after Father died, I
haven't been able to tell anyone half of the things
we carried around in that old car and couldn't say;
and there are people now I couldn't confront, even this far,
without dislodging everything in the West.

A new time is here now; I have come back,
and though I speak with less noise
all the little clods lie stunned with effort to remember,
for again it is tumbleweed time; they come to
judge us again. I know that the weakness we blame in ourselves
is in the judgment we use: I know what I remember wheels
endlessly here to say the same thing. And I know it is time
to cut loose off downwind free
like the eagles that keep the mountains clean.

The Farm on the Great Plains

A telephone line goes cold;
birds tread it wherever it goes.
A farm back of a great plain
tugs an end of the line.

I call that farm every year,
ringing it, listening, still;
no one is home at the farm,
the line gives only a hum.

Some year I will ring the line
on a night at last the right one,
and with an eye tapered for braille
from the phone on the wall

I will see the tenant who waits—
the last one left at the place;
through the dark my braille eye
will lovingly touch his face.

"Hello, is Mother at home?"
No one is home today.
"But Father—he should be there."
No one—no one is here.

"But you—are you the one . . . ?"
Then the line will be gone
because both ends will be home:
no space, no birds, no farm.

My self will be the plain,
wise as winter is gray,
pure as cold posts go
pacing toward what I know.

Listening

My father could hear a little animal step,
or a moth in the dark against the screen,
and every far sound called the listening out
into places where the rest of us had never been.

More spoke to him from the soft wild night
than came to our porch for us on the wind;
we would watch him look up and his face go keen
till the walls of the world flared, widened.

My father heard so much that we still stand
inviting the quiet by turning the face,
waiting for a time when something in the night
will touch us too from that other place.

II

The Well Rising

The well rising without sound,
the spring on a hillside,
the plowshare brimming through deep ground
everywhere in the field—

The sharp swallows in their swerve
flaring and hesitating
hunting for the final curve
coming closer and closer—

The swallow heart from wing beat to wing beat
counseling decision, decision:
thunderous examples. I place my feet
with care in such a world.

At the Bomb Testing Site

At noon in the desert a panting lizard
waited for history, its elbows tense,
watching the curve of a particular road
as if something might happen.

It was looking for something farther off
than people could see, an important scene
acted in stone for little selves
at the flute end of consequences.

There was just a continent without much on it
under a sky that never cared less.
Ready for a change, the elbows waited.
The hands gripped hard on the desert.

At the Chairman's Housewarming

Talk like a jellyfish can ruin a party.
It did: I smiled whatever they said,
all the time wanting to assert myself
by announcing to all, "I eat whole wheat bread."

The jelly talk stole out on the cloth
and coated the silver tine by tine,
folding meek spoons and the true knifeblades
and rolling a tentacle into the wine.

And my talk too—it poured on the table
and coiled and died in the sugar bowl,
twitching a last thin participle
to flutter the candle over its soul.

Nothing escaped the jellyfish,
that terror from seas where whales can't live
(he could kill sharks by grabbing their tails
and neither refusing nor consenting to give).

Oh go home, you terrible fish;
let sea be sea and rock be rock.
Go back wishy-washy to your sheltered bay,
but let me live definite, shock by shock.

When I Was Young

That good river that flowed backward
when it felt the danger of Babylon
taught the rest of us in the story how to be good,
but my mother said, "God, I used to love that town."

Animals that knew the way to Heaven
wagged at the back doors of every house
when I was young, and horses told fences
the story of Black Beauty, and smelled of the good manger.

Those times tested the pre-war clocks, and
cold mornings they rang and rang. I haven't recently
seen rivers flow backward or animals that remember.
The clocks, though, still pursue what they endlessly loved.

Doubt on the Great Divide

One of the lies the world is compelled to tell
is that God grips boards by thought into Plato's table.
Better to stand in the dark of things and crash,
hark yourself, blink in the day, eat bitter bush
and look out over the world. A steadfast wire
shaking off birds into the paralyzed air
crosses the country; in the sound of noon you stand
while tethers whisper out and come to their end.

Mountains that thundered promises now say something small—
wire in the wind, and snow beginning to fall.

Winterward

Early in March we pitched our scar,
this fact of a life, in dust;
in summer there was a green alarm,
a foxfire of fear, the distrust
of sighting under a willow tree
a little eggshell, burst.

It was mostly quiet, but threatenings
flared wherever we looked;
in autumn the birds fell to the ground
and crawled away to the rocks;
no sleep at night for anyone,
we stared at a moon like chalk.

Now we hear the stars torn upward
out of the sky; the alarm
shadows us as we run away
from this fact of a life, our home.
Oh winter, oh snowy interior,
rocks and hurt birds, we come.

The Epitaph Ending in And

In the last storm, when hawks
blast upward and a dove is
driven into the grass, its broken wings
a delicate design, the air between
wracked thin where it stretched before,
a clear spring bent close too often
(that Earth should ever have such wings
burnt on in blind color!), this will be
good as an epitaph:

Doves did not know where to fly, and

Keepsakes

Star Guides:
    Any star is enough
    if you know what star it is.

Kids:
    They dance before they learn
    there is anything that isn't music.

The Limbs of the Pin Oak Tree:
    "Gravity—what's that?"

An Argument Against the Empirical Method:
    Some haystacks don't even have any needle.

Comfort:
    We think it is calm here,
    or that our storm is the right size.

A Documentary from America

When the Presidential candidate came to our town
he had used up his voice, but he delivered a speech
written by a committee, through a friend of his
running on the same ticket. The candidate smiled.
We cheered his courage, and a cynic hissed:
"Fools, you are on TV and have just helped elect that man!"

Later at a motel in Nanton, Alberta
(a town on the plains with a special surprise—
a pipe that gushes a drink like a flash by the road),
we tuned in a show with a variety of plots
to stalk viewers with (whereas Westerns had only
to open up with one, say a .44) there in the twilight.

In the midst of a commercial we had democratically
elected and now found delivered forever on the screen,
we were interrupted to learn we had just won a war,
certified by experts to be correct. We felt at ease,
conscience a subliminal bonus, delivered
by flags and that eerie music when the enemy appeared.

Then there was our candidate smiling at our crowd,
just as an interviewer invaded our motel to ask what program
we were watching. "Oh God," we said, "we were watching
us, watching us." And in a terrible voice he roared,
"Quick, be smiling; you are on the air again!" and—
a terrible thing—we said just as he said, "How do you do."

Out West

This air the mountains watch, in Oregon, holds
every flower or tree embraced. You meet
the air at the door and stop: it has brought
waterfalls in its breath. Kids call, dogs bark,
a chain saw climbs the latticework behind the trees.

We know each day by the space it has
and then what fills it. There is a reward
here—maybe the mountains, maybe only the sense
that after what is must come something else, always.
It's a light thing, a bounce, to live here.

At Salem we saw Governor Hatfield
wave his hand: his arm was
the taffy Oregon pulled, and his voice
was drawn by invisible birds as far
as geese bob in the reeds near Klamath Falls.

The Oregon day crowds in at the door,
its cool air and the smell of rain brought
all over as we tremble to smell
the fog in its paw, our breath moving to get
loose in the woods or over the restless water.

And in the mountains that water is clear,
only a reminder of the air it looks at;
the trout hang there on their little
fin wings, hearing the Governor speak into the
microphone spots on their applauding gills.

At This Point on the Page

Frightened at the slant of the writing, I looked up
at the student who shared it with me—
such pain was in the crossing of each t,
and a heart that skipped—lurched—in the loop of the y.
Sorrowing for the huddled lines my eyes had seen—
the terror of the o's and a's, and those draggled g's,
I looked up at her face,
not wanting to read farther, at least by prose:
the hand shook that wrote that far on the page,
and what weight formed each word, God knows.

In the Deep Channel

Setting a trotline after sundown
if we went far enough away in the night
sometimes up out of deep water
would come a secret-headed channel cat,

Eyes that were still eyes in the rush of darkness,
flowing feelers noncommittal and black,
and hidden in the fins those rasping bone daggers,
with one spiking upward on its back.

We would come at daylight and find the line sag,
the fishbelly gleam and the rush on the tether:
to feel the swerve and the deep current
which tugged at the tree roots below the river.

Connections

Ours is a low, curst, under-swamp land
the raccoon puts his hand in,
gazing through his mask for tendrils
that will hold it all together.

No touch can find that thread, it is too small.
Sometimes we think we learn its course—
through evidence no court allows
a sneeze may glimpse us Paradise.

But ways without a surface we can find
flash through the mask only by surprise—
a touch of mud, a raccoon smile.

And if we purify the pond, the lilies die.

At the Fair

Even the flaws were good—

The fat lady defining the thin man
and both bracketing the bareback princess;

Ranging through the crowd the clown
taking us all in, being extreme;

And the swain with the hangdog air
putting his trust in popcorn and cotton candy.

What more could anyone ask?
We had our money's worth.

And then besides, outside the gate,
for nothing, we met one of those lithe women—

The whirling girl, laughing with a crooked old man.

Passing Remark

In scenery I like flat country.
In life I don't like much to happen.

In personalities I like mild colorless people.
And in colors I prefer gray and brown.

My wife, a vivid girl from the mountains,
says, "Then why did you choose me?"

Mildly I lower my brown eyes—
there are so many things admirable people
    do not understand.

The Fish Counter at Bonneville

Downstream they have killed the river and built a dam;
by that power they wire to here a light:
a turbine strides high poles to spit its flame
at this flume going down. A spot glows white
where an old man looks on at the ghosts of the game
in the flickering twilight—deep dumb shapes that glide.

So many Chinook souls, so many silverside.

Walking West

Anyone with quiet pace who
walks a gray road in the West
may hear a badger underground where
in deep flint another time is

Caught by flint and held forever,
the quiet pace of God stopped still.
Anyone who listens walks on
time that dogs him single file,

To mountains that are far from people,
the face of the land gone gray like flint.
Badgers dig their little lives there,
quiet-paced the land lies gaunt,

The railroad dies by a yellow depot,
town falls away toward a muddy creek.
Badger-gray the sod goes under
a river of wind, a hawk on a stick.

At the Klamath Berry Festival

The war chief danced the old way—
the eagle wing he held before his mouth—
and when he turned the boom-boom
stopped. He took two steps. A sociologist
was there; the Scout troop danced.
I envied him the places where he had not been.

The boom began again. Outside he heard
the stick game, and the Blackfoot gamblers
arguing at poker under lanterns.
Still-moccasined and bashful, holding
the eagle wing before his mouth,
listening and listening, he danced after others stopped.

He took two steps, the boom caught up,
the mountains rose, the still deep river
slid but never broke its quiet.
I looked back when I left:
he took two steps, he took two steps,
past the sociologist.

Near Edinburgh Castle

Wind riffles a telephone book;
rain falls on a name, maybe some president
who believes in himself and his cabinet
   —now elected by the mist.

Later, the book falls apart;
names mumble "Here," then fade.
What rain, mist, or snow elect
    they then contest into the ground.

Arrived at the castle, at the top,
in the chapel, white stone inside,
we tourists and the guard read a list
   —those dead in the war, the drowned.

My hearing catches at the wind
where it worries the flag overhead
and wears away stone while we read,
    "Their only grave is the sea."

Our People

Under the killdeer cry
our people hunted all day
graying toward winter, their lodges
thin to the north wind's edge.

Watching miles of marsh grass
take the supreme caress,
they looked out over the earth,
and the north wind felt like the truth.

Fluttering in that wind
they stood there on the world,
clenched in their own lived story
under the killdeer cry.

III

Following the *Markings* of Dag Hammarskjöld:

A GATHERING OF POEMS IN THE SPIRIT OF HIS LIFE AND WRITINGS

Prologue

You have to take the road seriously
even if it promises only perspective,
and listen to how songs learn any country,
how they arch over the snow, round out from windows,
and oh, take back the less than song, the willows
that say please, the plow lines overworked
horses leave on the field and on your mind.

These are reminders I do not care to live by,
the apparent rain, the days that forgot all
but their being, the way we leaned in the swing,
our soft arrival in the dusk when the lights
met our distance, and the lights were farms,
or stars, or trains; the lines of street lights
that came on saying "Zing."

What we bring back is what we derive from
our errors: we sweep over the ground
our detectors that show where there aren't
any mines; we stamp the earth and cry
"Betrayed—not exploded, but welcomed—a trick!"
Something has folded into this weather, the gush
a mushroom caused, and all damp land becomes
clung everywhere as the hand tries to let go.
So I try not to learn, disengage because reasons
block the next needed feeling. While others
talk, all of my tentative poems begin
to open their eyes, wistful: they could

grow better! And none carry enough
the burden you lifted, to know for us,
to fear, to act, and just to be.

A Song Demonstrators in Mexico Sing in Troubled Parts of a City

Dear ones, watching us on any street,
we come in from the country where we were alone,
and all your faces charm us, make us weep,
for the little world we share, our various home.

Think of us in Aguascalientes
listening to sad music while the rain
finds every mistake in the masonry
and caverns under the city echo ancient wrong.

We have walked those miles that make a nation,
all its hills the color of the wind,
and what we passed solicits us for kindness:
we bring you greeting from that land.

Mockingbirds can't imitate baby quail
silent in fear, quiet as a leaf,
but have to match their shadows on a stone;
and we, the poor from the country, who will soon be gone,

Bring into your whirlwind a memory of stillness,
lifted a moment and carried through the town
to honor that cavern joining all of us,
the common humanity country and city own.

A Thanksgiving for My Father

"The freezing convict wanted
back in the prison. The warden

laughed and let the storm execute
him. The wind mourned."

How often such abrupt
flakes formed around us!—
jabs of ice into lace,
daggers that appeared out of nothing,

So graceful the heart beat
late, could never catch up
again. You imagined a face in the
snow to burn the furnace down, and

"Once a wolf brought sticks
to a beaver—the mountains are
surely that big." Oh father, why
did you ever set your son such being!

Your life was a miracle
and could build out of shadows
anything: your restless thought
has made the world haunted;

Your memory like a snowflake forms
out of the night and comes down like
a new star all the time over wolf, storm,
woods, and millions of faces. . . .

"Once a child named 'Remember'
found a forest that wasn't trees, except
for one—named 'Doris Pine.' . . ."
Oh father, you always found the way,

But even Doris—I've never found her.

Jack London

Teeth meet on a jugular, pause, and bite:
all the world turns red but the falling snow,
and oh how quiet the river holds its flow
by one bank, then another—the vise of rock
and the force of summer fighting far below.

Another time, on an island, wedge birds
come, welcome to fly and exercise their song
on what divides all hope from land;
the sky holds where it is, but ready to move
when the forest answers softly after a storm:

He found such furs for the cold, called "Beauty,"
and "Courage" that fell through the ice, and a dog so wild
it howls the mountains higher, that howled
ages ago for us to come to the North
and exercise our song, from the island world.

The Concealment: Ishi, the Last Wild Indian

A rock, a leaf, mud, even the grass
Ishi the shadow man had to put back where it was.
In order to live he had to hide that he did.
His deep canyon he kept unmarked for the world,
and only his face became lined, because no one saw it
and it therefore didn't make any difference.

It he appeared, he died; and he was the last. Erased
footprints, berries that purify the breath, rituals
before dawn with water—even the dogs roamed a land
unspoiled by Ishi, who used to own it, with his aunt
and uncle, whose old limbs bound in willow bark finally
stopped and were hidden under the rocks, in sweet leaves.

We ought to help change that kind of premature suicide,
the existence gradually mottled away till the heartbeat
blends and the messages all go one way from the world
and disappear inward: Ishi lived. It was all right
for him to make a track. In California now where his opposites
unmistakably dwell we wander their streets

And sometimes whisper his name—
"Ishi."

Glimpses in the Woods

"Don't you want people to think well of you?"
"No—give them things, and then disappear."

That yew tree in the woods, that hermit,
that giver of bows, drinker of shade
with limbs far stronger than any need
being light, airy, and conservative,
offers a sudden glimpse out far—

That yew tree down a corridor
no one plans—useless for lumber, not even a weed,
a millionaire of disregard. Miles deep,
this earth will be rich after our time,
and yew trees quietly link through the woods. . . .

In the cold woods, I looked for this place—
beside the road and far up in the cold woods:
listeners, you have met sincere men and pretenders—
all I say is I was there and am here. Let me be
remembered only for the mud on my hands.

Listeners, I have come far to keep it from
making a difference whether I lie or

tell the truth: if incidents of my journey
sing right for you, then my mouth can abide
this communion, or I can gnaw other bones.

What ponds realize in the rain, or all of
that neglect the wilderness pours into the sky
lacking any viewer after Labor Day,
I think that, and can save it—from one glance
deep through fir woods at one dark tree;

And now into its corridor like a question,
a tunnel with one end, a mine meant
to escape from the dark, the tall days go on,
go down, and there I fall, freed on a new
level—beginning to learn for my life!

Let any feather or branch on the wind occur,
and a wind that polished the stars teach me
indifference. I have known with an edge too
clear. Yew tree, make me steadfast in my
weakness: teach me the sacred blur.

Walking the Wilderness

God is never sure He has found
the right grass. It never forgets Him.
My mother in a dream dreamed
this place, where storms drown
down or where God makes it arch to mountains,
flood with winter, stare upward at His
eye that freezes people, His zero breath
their death. In the night they lie, she
dreamed, sealed with lips to earth, who wait
at last with confidence for justice
or such firm coming as the wolverine's.

All the way into her dream and back
I walk and guard the day, since daylight broke
past guards of trees and streamed away.
Hear me, full sky, all your
lines I do not know, the roads
birds fly, the channels their lives make—
my mother in the dream dreamed
even deeper: people drowned awake,
each one staring, alone, pitiable,
come to all at once in that
dream, welcomed the more, the more
they trembled. God never notices opposition;
the deep of that dream always waits.

Snowflake designs lock; they clasp in the sky,
hold their patterns one by one, down,
spasms of loneliness, each one God's answer.
Warm human representatives may vote and
manage man; but last the blizzard will dignify
the walker, the storm hack trees to cyclone
groves, he catch the snow, his brave eye
become command, the whole night howl against
his ear, till found by dawn he
reach out to God no trembling hand.

IV

Bi-focal

Sometimes up out of this land
a legend begins to move.
Is it a coming near
of something under love?

Love is of the earth only,
the surface, a map of roads
leading wherever go miles
or little bushes nod.

Not so the legend under,
fixed, inexorable,
deep as the darkest mine
the thick rocks won't tell.

As fire burns the leaf
and out of the green appears
the vein in the center line
and the legend veins under there,

So, the world happens twice—
once what we see it as;
second it legends itself
deep, the way it is.

Right Now

Tonight in our secret town
wires are down. Black
lights along the street blow
steady in a wind held still.
A deaf dog listens. A girl
retreats from her gaze: her eyes
go endlessly back, a spool of shadow.

Led by my own dark I go
my unmarked everlasting round
frozen in this moment: Now
smooths all the smother, held,
wild but still. I know
so well nothing moves, arrived:
my glimpse, this town, our time.

From Eastern Oregon

Your day self shimmers at the mouth of a desert cave;
then you leave the world's problem and find
your own kind of light at the pool that glows far back
where the eye says it is dark. On the cave wall
you make not a shadow but a brightness; and you can feel
with your hands the carved story now forgotten or ignored
   by the outside, obvious mountains.

Your eyes an owl, your skin a new part of the earth,
you let obsidian flakes in the dust discover your feet
while somewhere drops of water tell a rock.
You climb out again and, consumed by light, shimmer
full contemporary being, but so thin your bones
register a skeleton along the rocks like
   an intense, interior diamond.

You carry the cave home, past Black Butte,
along the Santiam. The whole state
rides deep, and the swell of knowing it makes
yearning kelp of all you can't see.
For days your friends will be juniper, but
never again will material exist enough, clear—
   not any day, not here.

Once Men Were Created

A whistle had already loomed, outside
all encompassed ways, and its blade
hurt the ears of the dogs, then a slide
past the ears of even the sleeping men
and they were awake drowning in something
only the deaf could swim.

Some thought it was only morning, or water;
a few held their ears and ran, but it just got louder.
One hoped and flooded his head and welcomed
every leaf and tap and the whole siren of the world.
But they all crazed fell,
checked and crystallized and cold.

At the time of that cruelest music now, at age fifteen,
my schoolroom sang and almost overtopped the sound,
but our Principal came. The girl beside me
bit her fingernails, and well she might, caught helpless
that year in a room in a song in a jangle
that buffeted her dress.

Oh smooth animals that swim your easy
sound, nervous only to catch a meal or a mate—
there is another level of your mild sound, and it
scrapes with a fingernail; it has its whelps in a cave;
deeper than anyone knows it arches cathedrals,
and sends anthems like this over the grave.

Ice-fishing

Not thinking other than how the hand works
I wait until dark here on the cold
world rind, ice-curved over simplest rock,
where the tugged river flows over hidden
springs too insidious to be quite forgotten.

When the night comes I plunge my hand
where the string of fish know their share
of the minimum. Then, bringing back my hand
is a great sunburst event; and slow
home with me over unmarked snow

In the wild flipping warmth of won-back thought
my boots, my hat, my body go.

A Human Condition

If there is a forest anywhere
the one you live with whimpers in her
sleep or construes a glance wrong, awake:
without intent she falls toward zero
impact; like an indicator on a chart
she rounds into terror, and the wild trees
try for her throat,
    if there is a forest anywhere.

If you concur with a world that has forests
in it, the one you live with will indict
you. If you like a farm, it will threaten.
Some people casually help each other:
if one likes a place the other finds
a kind going out of the breath at evening there.
    At your house any forest is everywhere.

But there are farms—to see them in the evening
extends your breath; you hover their hills
with regard for a world that offers human beings
a lavish, a deepening abode, in the evening,
like them. These places could have been home,
are lost to you now. They are foreign but good.
    There are these farms.

Across the Lake's Eye

Walking ice across the lake's eye
to the deep and looking along the sight
at other worlds asleep for space
but not for light—
we came wide awake.
"Why close what eyes we have?" you said,

And "There's a left-hand world that other people see
that slinks aside from me,
that my dog hears;
the negative of the world, that suicides love;
that comes along the track from its pinpoint place;
that barely swerves beside our face
escaping either way outside our own,
beyond where night surprises the snow."

You made me look around that night.
And coming back you spun this left-hand story:
An island burrowed under the water
and rose pretending to be a different island
but a fish had followed it, making bubbles
wherever the island went. "Echoes,"
you said, "avoid that island now:
sound is dead there, but haunts the concave water
where the island used to be."

The world has character, you contended,
as we stamped home across the land,
making a record of that night,
marking the progress of an island.

For the Grave of Daniel Boone

The farther he went the farther home grew.
Kentucky became another room;
the mansion arched over the Mississippi;
flowers were spread all over the floor.
He traced ahead a deepening home,
and better, with goldenrod:

Leaving the snakeskin of place after place,
going on—after the trees
the grass, a bird flying after a song.
Rifle so level, sighting so well
his picture freezes down to now,
a story-picture for children.

They go over the velvet falls
into the tapestry of his time,
heirs to the landscape, feeling no jar:
it is like evening; they are the quail
surrounding his fire, coming in for the kill;
their little feet move sacred sand.

Children, we live in a barbwire time
but like to follow the old hands back—
the ring in the light, the knuckle, the palm,
all the way to Daniel Boone,
hunting our own kind of deepening home.
From the land that was his I heft this rock.

Here on his grave I put it down.

Hunting

What the keen hound followed
rose in the mind for me
taller for being faint, brought
near by what might be,
till—reversal—through the world
I found so misty a trail
that all not you cried, "You!"
like a wedding bell.

Bugles that fade are still bugles;
birds that sang wait still:
deep in the woods is that far place
once near, and our own, and real.

The Move to California

1   *The Summons in Indiana*

In the crept hours on our street
(repaired by snow that winter night)
from the west an angel of blown newspaper
was coming toward our house out of the dark.

Under all the far streetlights
and along all the near housefronts
silence was painting what it was given
that in that instant I was to know.

Starting up, mittened by sleep, I thought
of the sweeping stars and the wide night,
remembering as well as I could the hedges
back home that minister to comprehended fields—

And other such limits to hold the time near,
for I felt among strangers on a meteor
trying to learn their kind of numbers
to scream together in a new kind of algebra.

That night the angel went by in the dark,
but left a summons: Try farther west.
And it did no good to try to read it again:
there are things you cannot learn through manyness.

2   *Glimpsed on the Way*

Think of the miles we left,
and then the one slow cliff
coming across the north,
and snow.

From then on, wherever north was,
hovering over us
always it would go,
everywhere.

I wander that desert yet
whenever we draw toward night.
Somewhere ahead that cliff
still goes.

3   *At the Summit*

Past the middle of the continent—
wheatfields turning in God's hand
green to pale to yellow,
like the season gradual—
we approached the summit
prepared to face the imminent
map of all our vision,
the sudden look at new land.

As we stopped there, neutral,
standing on the Great Divide,
alpine flora, lodgepole pine
fluttering down on either side—
a little tree just three feet high
shared our space between the clouds,
opposing all the veering winds.
Unhurried, we went down.

4   *Springs Near Hagerman*

Water leaps from lava near Hagerman,
piles down riverward over rock
reverberating tons of exploding shock
   out of that stilled world.

We halted there once. In that cool
we drank, for back and where we had to go
lay our jobs and Idaho,
    lying far from such water.

At work when I vision that sacred land—
the vacation of mist over its rock wall—
I go blind with hope. That plumed fall
    is bright to remember.

5   *Along Highway 40*

Those who wear green glasses through Nevada
travel a ghastly road in unbelievable cars
and lose pale dollars
under violet hoods when they park at gambling houses.

I saw those martyrs—all sure of their cars in the open
and always believers in any handle they pulled—
wracked on an invisible cross
and staring at a green table.

While the stars were watching
I crossed the Sierras in my old Dodge
letting the speedometer measure God's kindness,
and slept in the wilderness on the hard ground.

6   *Written on the Stub of the First Paycheck*

Gasoline makes game scarce.
In Elko, Nevada, I remember a stuffed wildcat
someone had shot on Bing Crosby's ranch.
I stood in the filling station
breathing fumes and reading the snarl of a map.

There were peaks to the left so high
they almost got away in the heat;

Reno and Las Vegas were ahead.
I had promise of the California job,
and three kids with me.

It takes a lot of miles to equal one wildcat
today. We moved into a housing tract.
Every dodging animal carries my hope in Nevada.
It has been a long day, Bing.
Wherever I go is your ranch.

Sophocles Says

History is a story God is telling,
by means of hidden meanings written closely
inside the skins of things. Far over the sun
lonesome curves are meeting, and in the clouds
birds bend the wind. Hunting a rendezvous,
soft as snowflakes ride through a storm their pattern down,
men hesitate a step, touched by home.

A man passes among strangers; he never smiles;
the way a flame goes begging among the trees
he goes, and he suffers, himself, the kind of dark
that anything sent from God experiences,
until he finds through trees the lights of a town—
a street, the houses blinded in the rain—
and he hesitates a step, shocked—at home.

For God will take a man, no matter where,
and make some scene a part of what goes on:
there will be a flame; there will be a snowflake form;
and riding with the birds, wherever they are,
bending the wind, finding a rendezvous
beyond the sun or under the earth—that man
will hesitate a step—and meet his home.

Near

Walking along in this not quite prose way
we both know it is not quite prose we speak,
and it is time to notice this intolerable snow
innumerably touching, before we sink.

It is time to notice, I say, the freezing snow
hesitating toward us from its gray heaven;
listen—it is falling not quite silently
and under it still you and I are walking.

Maybe there are trumpets in the houses we pass
and a redbird watching from an evergreen—
but nothing will happen until we pause
to flame what we know, before any signal's given.

The Animal That Drank Up Sound

1

One day across the lake where echoes come now
an animal that needed sound came down. He gazed
enormously, and instead of making any, he took
away from, sound: the lake and all the land
went dumb. A fish that jumped went back like a knife,
and the water died. In all the wilderness around he
drained the rustle from the leaves into the mountainside
and folded a quilt over the rocks, getting ready
to store everything the place had known; he buried—
thousands of autumns deep—the noise that used to come there.

Then that animal wandered on and began to drink
the sound out of all the valleys—the croak of toads,
and all the little shiny noise grass blades make.
He drank till winter, and then looked out one night
at the stilled places guaranteed around by frozen
peaks and held in the shallow pools of starlight.
It was finally tall and still, and he stopped on the highest
ridge, just where the cold sky fell away
like a perpetual curve, and from there he walked on silently,
and began to starve.

When the moon drifted over that night the whole world lay
just like the moon, shining back that still
silver, and the moon saw its own animal dead
on the snow, its dark absorbent paws and quiet
muzzle, and thick, velvet, deep fur.

2

After the animal that drank sound died, the world
lay still and cold for months, and the moon yearned

and explored, letting its dead light float down
the west walls of canyons and then climb its delighted
soundless way up the east side. The moon
owned the earth its animal had faithfully explored.
The sun disregarded the life it used to warm.

But on the north side of a mountain, deep in some rocks,
a cricket slept. It had been hiding when that animal
passed, and as spring came again this cricket waited,
afraid to crawl out into the heavy stillness.
Think how deep the cricket felt, lost there
in such a silence—the grass, the leaves, the water,
the stilled animals all depending on such a little
thing. But softly it tried—"Cricket!"—and back like a river
from that one act flowed the kind of world we know,
first whisperings, then moves in the grass and leaves;
the water splashed, and a big night bird screamed.

It all returned, our precious world with its life and sound,
where sometimes loud over the hill the moon,
wild again, looks for its animal to roam, still,
down out of the hills, any time.
But somewhere a cricket waits.

It listens now, and practices at night.

Recoil

The bow bent remembers home long,
the years of its tree, the whine
of wind all night conditioning
it, and its answer—Twang!

To the people here who would fret me down
their way and make me bend:
By remembering hard I could startle for home
and be myself again.

Read to the Last Line

Suppose a heroic deed—
at a big picnic, say, you save a child;
later the child is killed while being a hero;
then you meet the beautiful sister,
and all . . . ; you have a son who wakes
in the middle of the night and cries;
you hear him—strange—there in the dark, and—

Suppose all the supposes.
You find your self-story patch-quilted
all over the place; and after that
you are reading an author who tells
your whole story, around all the spirals,
till you come face to face and recognize you.

Grateful, you find yourself
identified, so clearly named that you decide
to bring other patches together by
rounding on that author, too, with some
greatest, ultimate deed; he deserves something.

So you in turn begin a story,
but then you stop—what goes on?
"I'll not tell nor be told what I think," you cry,
"None of it's true, anyway."

And all the time it's your own story,
even when you think: "It's all just made up, a trick.
What is the author trying to do?"

Reader, we are in such a story:
all of this is trying to arrange a kind of a prayer for you.

Pray for me.

About the Author

William Stafford was born in Hutchinson, Kansas. He lived there until high-school age, when his father's job took the family to other Kansas towns, where they used to fish and camp and explore and haunt the library. "A family ritual was the evening walk to exchange the read for the unread; we would stroll along, each member of the family with an armload of books."

Mr. Stafford received his B.A. and M.A. at the University of Kansas and his doctorate at the State University of Iowa. His poetry has appeared in many magazines, among them the *Atlantic Monthly*, *Harper's*, *The New Yorker* and *The Nation*, and in numerous anthologies. His first poetry collection was *West of Your City*, published in 1960. In 1962 Harper & Row published *Traveling through the Dark*, which received the National Book Award for the most distinguished work of poetry by an American author. In 1964, he was given the Shelley Memorial Award of the Poetry Society of America, and he received an honorary D. Lit. degree from Ripon College in June, 1965.

Mr. Stafford lives in Lake Oswego, Oregon, with his wife and four children. Since 1948 he has taught English literature and composition at Lewis and Clark College in Portland, Oregon. A Guggenheim Foundation Award for the academic year 1966–1967 will enable him to "stay home and write"—an exuberant prospect.